Middle Ages
Reference Library
Cumulative Index

Middle Ages
Ages
Reference Library
Cumulative Index

Cumulates Indexes For:

Middle Ages: Almanac
Middle Ages: Biographies
Middle Ages: Primary Sources

Judy Galens,
Index Coordinator

AN IMPRINT OF THE GALE GROUP

DETROIT · NEW YORK · SAN FRANCISCO
LONDON · BOSTON · WOODBRIDGE, CT

Middle Ages Reference Library: Cumulative Index

Staff

Judy Galens, *Index Coordinator*
Pamela A. E. Galbreath, *Senior Art Director*
Kenn Zorn, *Product Design Manager*

Marco Di Vita, Graphix Group, *Typesetting*

ISBN 0-7876-5575-9

The front cover photograph of crusaders disembarking in Egypt was reproduced by permission of the Corbis Corporation.

Printed in the United States of America

10 9 8 7 6 5 4 3 2 1

Middle Ages Reference Library Cumulative Index

A=Middle Ages: Almanac
B=Middle Ages: Biographies
PS=Middle Ages: Primary Sources

Bold type indicates set title, main entries, and their page numbers.

Italic type indicates volume numbers.

Illustrations are marked by (ill.).

Arabs
A 5, 6, 50, 63–65, 69–74,
80, 102, 127, 139, 145,
146, 209
B *1:* 37, 44, 163, 189, *2:*
213, 257, 258, 321, 322
PS 2, 16–18, 142
Aragon
A 219
B *1:* 99, 100, 174
Archaeology
A 172, 186, 188, 195, 196
Archbishop of Canterbury
A 107, 114
B *1:* 114–16, 142, *2:* 314
Archbishops
PS 114
Architecture
A 4, 30, 35, 36, 54, 55, 69,
74, 110–12, 113, 142,
205, 220
B *1:* 64, 175, *2:* 204, 365,
368
Arianism
A 12, 16, 25
B *1:* 79, 81, 142
PS 90, 94, 99
Arigböge
B *2:* 211
Aristocracy
A 20, 31, 178–80, 182
B *1:* 41
Aristotle
A 72, 129
B *1:* 31, 33–35, 35 (ill.),
37, 49, *2:* 226, 236, 351
Arius
A 12
Armenia
A 50, 59, 138
B *1:* 44, 134, *2:* 346
PS 6
Armenian Christians
A 104
Armor
A 5, 34, 38, 39, 110, 117,
120, 181, 217, 221–23
B *2:* 193, 194, 198, 248,
326
PS 71, 148
Arsuf
B *2:* 316, 327

Art
A 20, 28, 30, 48, 52–54,
62, 83, 110–13, 142,
162, 170, 178, 184, 189,
198, 221
Arthur (of England; leg-
endary king)
A 118–20
B *1:* 80, 81
PS 147, 156
Arthur of Anjou
B *1:* 109, 111
Artillery
A 108, 111
Artisans
PS 27, 48, 82, 84
Aryabhata
B *2:* 235, **236–37**, 238
Aryabhatiya
B *2:* 237
Ashikaga shogunate
A 183
B *1:* 57
Ashikaga Takauji
A 183
B *1:* 56
Ashkenazim
A 86, 90
Asia
A 12, 37, 47–51, 57, 59,
64, 75, 77, 80, 82, 104,
126, 131, 133–37, 142,
151–53, 155, 156, 164,
165, 167, 168, 171, 172,
175, 197, 214
B *1:* 10, 13, 14, 86, 125,
129, 130, 156, 187, *2:*
199, 209, 210, 212, 220,
221, 254, 258, 273, 274,
282, 292, 298, 300–03,
331, 332, 342, 344, 360
PS 1, 3, 15, 33, 34, 54, 74,
104, 105, 132
Asia Minor. *See also* Anato-
lia; Turkey
A 12, 47–49, 59, 77, 80,
104, 126
B *1:* 86, 187, *2:* 220, 273,
292, 298
Assassination
A 8, 68
B *1:* 117, *2:* 206

Assassins
A 69, 81, 136
B *2:* 316, 323, 361
Assyria
A 61
Astrology
A 122, 127, 189
B *1:* 69, 70, 94, 153, 154
PS 36, 39
Astronomy
A 34, 36, 72, 127, 167,
187–89
B *1:* 55, *2:* 237, 238, 240
Asturias
A 219
Asuka period
A 176
PS 103
Aswan
B *2:* 239
Atahualpa
A 198
Athanasius
B *2:* 204
Athens
B *1:* 4, 30, 96, 98, 112,
135, 166, 176, 185, 186,
2: 333, 342, 348, 360,
370
PS 130
Atlantic Ocean
A 9, 205
B *1:* 155, *2:* 254
Atlantis
A 158
Attila
A 16, 17, 37, 38, 42
Audovera
B *2:* 373
Augustine
A 4, 15, 16, 29, 65
B *1:* **23–30**, 23 (ill.), 53,
74, 121, 139, 143, 162,
179, *2:* 292
PS 53, **57–64**
Augustine of Canterbury
B *1:* 142
Australia
A 158
PS 151
Austria
A 19, 96, 124, 131, 218

B *1:* 17, 108, 135, *2:* 247, 315, 316, 318
PS 33
Austro-Hungarian Empire
B *1:* 19
Auxerre
B *2:* 291
Avalon
A 118
Avars
A 54, 78
Averroës
A 72, 127, 129
B *1:* **31–37,** 31 (ill.), 49, *2:* 227, 235, 350, 351
Avicenna
A 72, 127
B *1:* 49, *2:* 226–28, 227 (ill.), 235, 236, 239
Avignon
A 132, 222, 226
B *1:* 118, 183
PS 46, 47, 50, 124, 128
Axayacatl
B *2:* 254
Ayyubid dynasty
A 75
B *2:* 322
Azcapotzalco
A 192
Azerbaijan
B *2:* 345, 346
Azores
B *1:* 158
Aztec Empire
A 187, 190–94, 195, 196, 197, 198
B *2:* 251–56, 281

B

Babur
A 139, 149
B *2:* 347
Babylon
A 222
B *2:* 293
PS 128
Babylonia
A 61, 62
"Babylonian Captivity"
A 222

PS 128
Bacon, Roger
A 129
B *2:* 235, **240–41,** 241 (ill.)
Baffin Island
B *2:* 218, 219
Baghdad
A 70–72, 75, 79, 136, 138, 146
B *1:* 99, 103, 164, *2:* 213, 237, 238, 276, 307, 310
Bagrat III
A 139
Bagratid dynasty
A 139
B *1:* 44
Bajazed
A 83, 138
B *2:* 347
Balban
A 148
Baldwin of Boulogne
A 103
Bali
A 155
Balkan Peninsula
A 218
B *2:* 274, 275, 278, 318
Baltic Sea
A 41
B *1:* 16
Ban Kulin
B *2:* 274, 275
The Banquet
B *1:* 94
Bantu
A 201, 207–11
Barbarians
A 6, 9, 10, 13, 17, 28, 33, 48, 90, 134, 146, 161, 171, 172, 223
B *1:* 29, 36, 78, 166
PS 7, 16, 35, 94, 148, 155
Bardas Phocas
B *1:* 40–42
Bardas Sclerus
B *1:* 40–42
Bar Sauma, Rabban
B *2:* 213, 220
PS 41
"Base-10" system
A 146

Basil II
A 50, 53, 58, 59
B *1:* **39–45,** 39 (ill.), 58, 172, *2:* 230
Battle of ... *See* place names, for example, Hastings
Batu
A 135
B *1:* 16, 17
Baudricourt
B *2:* 193
Bavaria
A 34, 96
B *1:* 170, 180
PS 82
Bayeux Tapestry
A 95
B *2:* 369 (ill.)
PS 152
Bay of Bengal
B *2:* 301
Beatrice
B *1:* 91–93, 95
PS 122, 129
Becket, Thomas à
A 114, 116
B *1:* **115–17,** 116 (ill.), *2:* 314
Bede. *See* Venerable Bede
Bedouins
A 64
B *2:* 258
Beijing
A 134, 173
B *1:* 134, *2:* 209, 298–301, 303, 339
Belasitsa
A 59
Belgium
A 126
B *1:* 78, *2:* 221, 246, 360
Belgrade
A 104
Belisarius
A 48, 52
B *2:* 202, 203, 205
PS 135, 136, 140
Belize
A 185
Belle Isle
B *2:* 219
Benedict
A 25–27

B *1:* 178–79, 179 (ill.), 184, *2:* 350

Benedictine monks
A 27, 45
B *1:* 142

Benedictine Rule
B *1:* 179

Benin
A 211

Berengaria
B *2:* 315

Berenguer
B *1:* 101

Bernard of Clairvaux
A 109, 110
B *1:* 7, **47–52,** 47 (ill.), 51 (ill.), 105, 107, 292

Berne
PS 46, 47

Bible
A 24, 27–29, 73, 85, 87, 102, 113, 130, 224, 225
B *1:* 1, 4, 26, 28, 41, 74, 139, 150, 154, 162, 186, 187, *2:* 259, 290, 291
PS 15, 54, 95, 113, 124

Bingham, Hiram
A 196

Bishops
A 10, 12, 100, 101, 123, 132
B *1:* 145, 147
PS 90, 112, 114, 115

Bjarni Herjolfsson
B *2:* 218

Black Death
A 91, 213–15, 217, 218, 226
B *2:* 266, 361
PS 3, 43–45, 49–51

Black Guelphs
B *1:* 92

Black Sea
A 57, 58, 78, 79, 139, 214
B *2:* 301

Blues and Greens
A 52, 56
B *2:* 201
PS 137

Boccaccio, Giovanni
A 221
B *1:* 74, 119, *2:* 265–67, 267 (ill.), 270, 271

Boethius
B *1:* 41, **53–59,** 53 (ill.)

Bohemia
A 56, 99, 224
B *1:* 18, 19, 170

Bohemond
A 102, 103, 106
B *2:* 324, 325
PS 7–13

Bolivia
A 197

Bologna
B *1:* 69, 173, 178, 181

Boniface VIII (pope)
A 132, 222
B *1:* 140–41, 141 (ill.), 183
PS 124

Book of Changes in Fortune
B *1:* 72

Book of Kells
A 28

Book of Roger
B *2:* 220

The Book of Ser Marco Polo the Venetian Concerning the Kingdoms and Marvels of the East
B *2:* 302
PS 33–41

Book of the City of Ladies
B *1:* 73, 74

Book of the Deeds and Virtues of the Wise King Charles V
B *1:* 73

Book of the Duchess
B *1:* 118

Book of the Order of Chivalry
PS 87

Book of the Road of Long Study
B *1:* 73

Book of Three
B *1:* 74

Boris I
B *2:* 274

Borneo
A 155, 158

Borobudur
A 155

Borte
B *1:* 130, 131

Bosnia
A 83
B *1:* 19, *2:* 274, 275

Bosporus
A 104

Braveheart
B *2:* 196

Brendan
B *2:* 222

Brian Boru
B *1:* 132–33, 133 (ill.), 135

Britain
A 19, 21, 22, 39, 42, 92, 119. *See also* England
B *1:* 80, 114, 142, 162, *2:* 289, 290, 293. *See also* England
PS 145, 146, 151. *See also* England

British Isles
A 13, 28, 36, 39

Britons
A 21, 22, 118
B *1:* 80, 81
PS 145

Brittany
B *1:* 2, 3, 5, 7

Brunelleschi, Filippo
A 220

Brunhilda
PS 100

Buck, Pearl
PS 161

Buddha. *See* Siddhartha Gautama

Buddhism
A 66, 68, 141–45, 155, 162, 163, 166, 168, 170, 176, 178, 179, 183
B *2:* 284, 301, 329–31, 339
PS 67, 68, 91, 103–05, 161

Bulgaria
A 48, 50, 55, 59, 78, 82, 83, 104, 218
B *1:* 18, 88, 89, *2:* 274, 275, 279

Bulgars
A 50, 54, 55, 58, 78
B *1:* 16, *2:* 275

Burgundians
A 21, 30
PS 94, 98

PS 1, 5, 44, 50, 89, 90, 93,
111, 113, 124, 125, 128,
146, 149
Caucasus
A 83, 139
B *2:* 346
Cauchon, Peter
B *2:* 196
Cavalcanti, Guido
B *1:* 92
Cavalry
A 8, 14, 37, 50
B *2:* 244, 248
PS 148
Celestine V (pope)
B *1:* 140, 141
Celts
A 7, 13, 21
B *1:* 80, 81
PS 145
Cenotes
A 188
Central America
A 185, 186
Central Asia
A 77, 131, 133–35, 137,
164, 165, 168, 171, 172,
175
B *1:* 13, 129, 130, *2:* 209,
210, 221, 274, 298, 302,
331, 342, 344, 360
PS 1, 15, 33, 34, 74
Central Europe
A 90, 114
B *1:* 85, 89
Ceolfrid
B *1:* 162
Certaldo
B *2:* 267
Cervantes, Miguel de
A 222
B *2:* 265
Ceuta
B *1:* 154, 155
Ceylon
A 144–46, 172
B *1:* 10, 156, 157, 164, *2:*
301, 303
Chagatai
A 137
B *2:* 210, 213, 343, 344

Chain mail
A 34, 38, 39, 110. *See also*
Armor
Champa
A 152, 153
B *2:* 214, 301
Champagne
A 126
B *2:* 192
Ch'ang-an
A 167–69, 178–80
B *2:* 336
Chao Kou
B *2:* 338
Chao K'uang-yin
A 169
B *2:* 338
Chao Ping
B *2:* 339
Chapel of San Damiano
B *1:* 123
Charlemagne
A 31, 33–37, 39, 45, 53,
56, 93, 96, 97, 119
B *1:* **61–67,** 61 (ill.), 63
(ill.), 65 (ill.), 83, 99,
113, 114, 133, 146,
169–71, 185, 187, 189,
2: 204, 246, 274
PS 90, 99, 100, 111, 147
Charles V
B *1:* 69, 70, 73
PS 83
Charles VI
B *1:* 73
Charles VII
A 217
B *2:* 191, 193
Charles Martel
A 31, 33, 38, 93
B *1:* 62
PS 99
Charles of Anjou
PS 123
Charles the Bold
B *2:* 246–47, 247 (ill.)
Chartres
A 112, 113, 156
Chateau
A 108, 111
Chatillon
B *2:* 326

Chaucer, Geoffrey
A 221
B *1:* 59, 113, **118–19,** 118
(ill.), *2:* 267
PS 80
Chavín
A 185, 194
Cheng Ho
A 172, 209
B *1:* 156, 159, *2:* 220, 339
Childeric
B *1:* 78
Children's Crusade
A 124, 125
B *1:* 182
Chilperic
B *1:* 79, *2:* 373
PS 94, 98, 100
China
A 6, 14, 22, 70, 78, 127,
128, 134, 137, 138, 146,
151, 152, 154, 158,
161–74, 175, 178–81,
208, 209, 219, 225
B *1:* 4, 56, 129, 134, 156,
157, 159, 161, 164, 165,
188, 190, *2:* 209–15,
220, 267, 298–301, 303,
304, 329–32, 335–42,
347, 357–62, 371, 372,
374, 375
PS 3, 33–36, 38–41, 67,
76, 91, 103–05, 109,
155–57, 160, 161
Ch'in dynasty
A 161
Ch'in Shih Huang Ti
B *2:* 361
Chitor
A 149
Chivalry
A 2, 4, 5, 18, 32, 46, 106,
116, 119, 120, 132, 181,
226
PS 87, 100, 153
Chlodomir
B *1:* 79, 83
PS 95, 99, 100
Chlothar
B *2:* 373
Chola
B *1:* 10, 14

Comnena, Anna. *See* Anna Comnena

Comnenus, Alexis I. *See* Alexis I Comnenus

Compiègne
  B *1:* 2

Comprehensive Mirror for Aid in Chinese Government
  A 170

Concerning Famous Women
  B *1:* 74

Concordat of Worms
  B *1:* 115, 151

Confessions (Augustine)
  A 15
  B *1:* 23, 24, 28
  PS 53, 57–64

Confessions (Patrick)
  B *2:* 289, 290, 294, 295

Confucianism
  A 162, 164, 168, 170, 179
  B *1:* 4, *2:* 329, 331, 336
  PS 91, 104, 105

Confucius
  A 162, 164
  B *1:* 165, *2:* 331, 359
  PS 105

Congo
  A 208, 210, 211

Congo River
  A 210

Conrad III
  A 109
  B *1:* 172

Conrad of Montferrat
  B *2:* 316

Consolation of Philosophy
  B *1:* 53, 57, 59

Constans II
  A 50

Constantine
  A 11, 12, 16, 24, 36, 47, 53, 80
  B *2:* 293
  PS 89, 124, 125, 127

Constantine V
  A 53
  B *1:* 186

Constantine VI
  B *1:* 186, 187, 188

Constantinople. *See also* Istanbul
  A 12, 25, 41, 49–52, 54, 55, 83, 100, 104, 122, 126, 218
  B *1:* 86–89, 137, 138, 140, 158, 166, 167, 182, 186, 187, *2:* 199–201, 204, 205, 273, 275–78, 301, 353, 360
  PS 5, 8, 10–12, 139–42

Copernicus, Nicolaus
  B *2:* 237

Coptic
  A 25

Córdoba
  B *1:* 31, 34, 35, *2:* 224

Coroticus
  B *2:* 294

Cortés, Hernán
  A 194
  B *2:* 251

Cosmidion
  PS 7, 8

Council of Chalcedon
  A 25

Council of Clermont
  B *1:* 181

Council of Constance
  A 222, 224

Council of Ephesus
  A 25

Council of Florence
  A 203

Council of Nicaea
  A 12, 53

Council of Pisa
  A 222

Courtly love
  A 108, 119, 130
  B *1:* 72, 73, 119

Crane, Stephen
  PS 160

"The Cremation of Strasbourg Jewry, St. Valentine's Day, February 14, 1349—About the Great Plague and the Burning of the Jews"
  PS 43–51

Croatia
  A 50, 56
  B *1:* 19, *2:* 274

Crusaders
  A 81, 90, 104, 106, 110, 115, 116, 122–25, 127
  B *1:* 166, 167, 173, 182, *2:* 315, 316, 321, 322, 324, 326, 361

Crusader states
  A 104, 110
  B *1:* 181

Crusades. *See also* First Crusade, Second Crusade, etc.
  A 6, 72, 75, 80, 81, 90, 93, 99, 103, 106, 107, 110, 117, 120, 121, 124, 126, 127, 130, 132, 146, 203, 214, 220, 222
  B *1:* 52, 126, 152, 154, 167, 181, 182, *2:* 232, 240, 321, 324, 325, 328, 360, 361
  PS 2, 3, 10, 11, 12, 13, 15, 16, 21, 22, 86, 91, 119

Cumans
  A 79

Cupid
  B *1:* 73

Cuzco
  A 195, 197, 198
  B *2:* 282, 284, 286

Cyprus
  A 115
  B *2:* 315

Cyril
  A 55–57
  B *1:* 18, 42, **85–90**, 85 (ill.), *2:* 292

Cyrillic alphabet
  A 55–57
  B *1:* 85, 88

Czar
  A 59, 220
  B *1:* 21, 43, *2:* 274

Czech Republic
  A 55, 56
  B *1:* 18, 21, 86

D

Daigo II
  A 183

Daimyo
A 183
Dalai Lama
A 166
Damascus
A 70, 72, 110, 138
B *2:* 322, 327, 328
Danelaw
A 39
B *1:* 41
Danes
A 37, 39, 42
B *1:* 16, 40, 41, 132, 133
Daniel
B *1:* 2, 21, *2:* 249
Dante Alighieri
A 4, 221, 225
B *1:* 59, 73, **91–96,** 91
(ill.), 93 (ill.), 95 (ill.),
118, *2:* 227, 235, 266,
267, 328
PS 89, 91, **121–30**
Danube
A 9, 14
Dark Ages
A 2, 4, 5, 18, 69
B *1:* 83, 114, *2:* 353, 354,
375
David
B *1:* 45, *2:* 194, 224, 225,
249, 287, 304, 328
Decameron
A 221
B *2:* 265–67, 270
PS 80
Deccan Plateau
A 142, 146
B *1:* 10, 12
De Hauteville family
A 98, 101, 102. *See also*
Robert Guiscard
Delacroix, Eugène
B *1:* 93 (ill.)
Delhi
A 79, 138, 147–49
B *1:* 10, 11, 13, 14, *2:* 303,
347
Delhi Sultanate
A 79, 147
B *1:* 10, 11, 13, 14
De monarchia
B *1:* 94

Description of Africa
A 206
PS 23–31
Description of the World
B *2:* 302
Devagiri
B *1:* 12
De vulgari eloquentia
B *1:* 94
*Dialogue of a Philosopher with
a Jew and a Christian*
B *1:* 7
*The Diary of Lady
Sarashina*
PS 65–72
Diaspora
A 86, 87
Diocletian
A 11
B *2:* 293
Dionysius Exiguus
B *2:* 352
Diplomacy
A 48, 50, 124
B *2:* 283
Divan
A 78, 82
Divination
A 186, 198
Divine Comedy
A 221
B *1:* 73, 91–95, 95 (ill.)
PS 91, **121–30**
Divorce
A 67
B *1:* 105–07, *2:* 325
Djenné
B *2:* 248
Doctors
A 5, 71, 72, 146
B *1:* 139, *2:* 238, 239
PS 17, 161
Domesday Book
B *2:* 368, 370
Dominic
A 123
B *1:* 124, 125, 127, 183, *2:*
350
Dominican Order
A 123
B *1:* 125, 183, *2:* 350
Domremy
B *2:* 192

Donatello
A 221
Donation of Constantine
PS 125
Don Quixote
A 222
B *2:* 265
Dracula
B *2:* 346, 348
Dragon Throne
PS 158
Dublin
A 39
B *1:* 132
Duns Scotus, John
A 220
Dunyzad
PS 77
Durazzo
PS 7, 8

E

Early Middle Ages
A 2, 5, 19, 34, 36, 40, 42,
86, 99, 146
B *2:* 352
East Africa
A 209
B *2:* 339
East Asia
B *1:* 125, *2:* 212, 254, 332
PS 54, 105, 132
Easter
A 158
B *1:* 26, 51, 95, *2:* 293
PS 58, 122
Easter Island
A 158
Eastern Europe. *See also*
Byzantine Empire
A 1, 4, 21, 41, 42, 47–49,
56–59, 86, 99, 130, 134,
137, 218
B *1:* 18, 21, 86, 88, *2:* 210
PS 5
Eastern Orthodox Church
A 48, 55, 58, 59
B *1:* 16, 17, 44, 87, 88,
140, 186, 190
PS 5

Eastern Roman Empire. *See*
   Byzantine Empire
East Frankish Empire
   A 37
   B *2:* 246
East Indies
   A 158, 225
*Ecclesiastical History of the
   English People. See Histo-
   ria ecclesiastica gentis
   Anglorum*
Ecumenical councils
   A 12, 53, 100, 222
Eddas
   A 45
Edessa
   A 104, 109, 110
   B *1:* 50
Edirne
   A 82
Edward I
   A 92
   B *1:* 156, *2:* 196
Edward the Black Prince
   A 217
Edward the Confessor
   A 95
   B *2:* 367
   PS 146
Egypt
   A 12, 47, 48, 50, 61, 72,
      75, 79, 81, 82, 88, 115,
      122, 124, 126, 188, 193,
      201, 202, 205, 209
   B *1:* 32, 43, 164, *2:* 224,
      225, 232, 233, 239, 247,
      291, 322, 323, 325, 347
   PS 16, 17, 30, 140, 141
Einhard
   B *1:* 61, 64
Eisenstein, Sergei
   A 131
   B *1:* 19, 20
El Cid
   A 219
   B *1:* **97–103,** 97 (ill.), 164,
      181, 189
Eleanor of Aquitaine
   A 110, 114
   B *1:* **105–12,** 105 (ill.),
      116, 180, *2:* 314, 318
Eliot, T. S.
   B *2:* 309

Elizabeth I
   A 218
   B *1:* 59
El Mehmendar
   B *2:* 229
*Eloquence in the Vernacular
   Tongue*
   B *1:* 94
El Salvador
   A 185
Emma of Normandy
   B *2:* 367
England. *See also* Britain
   A 4, 22, 24, 28, 39–42, 92,
      95, 96, 107, 114–19,
      121, 124, 131, 132, 195,
      216–18, 222, 223, 225
   B *1:* 39–41, 59, 63, 80, 81,
      105, 108–14, 116, 120,
      140, 153, 161, 162, 170,
      174, 180, *2:* 191, 192,
      194, 196, 220, 240, 265,
      287, 293, 309, 313, 314,
      318, 319, 361, 365–69
   PS 118, 133, 145, 146,
      148–52
English Channel
   A 95, 216
English language
   A 98
   B *1:* 113, *2:* 368
   PS 151
**English scholars, thinkers,
   and writers**
   B *1:* 113–20
Enyu
   PS 68, 69
*Epistles on the Romance of the
   Rose*
   B *1:* 73
Epistle to the God of Love
   B *1:* 73
Eriksson, Leif. *See* Leif Eriks-
   son
Erik the Red
   B *2:* 217, 222
Erik the Red's Saga
   B *2:* 217, 222
Eritrea
   A 202
Ertogrul
   B *2:* 276

Estonians
   B *1:* 16
Ethelred the Unready
   A 95
   B *2:* 367
   PS 145
Ethics
   B *1:* 1, 7
Ethiopia
   A 201–03, 204
Étienne du Castel
   PS 83
Eucharist
   A 94, 101
Eugenius III (pope)
   A 109
   B *1:* 47, 50
Exodus
   B *2:* 224
Eyck, Jan van
   A 221
Ezana
   A 202
Ezekiel
   B *1:* 4

F

Falkirk
   B *2:* 196
Famine
   A 162, 169, 197
   B *1:* 124, 139, 141, *2:* 253
Fa Ngum
   A 154
Far East
   A 6, 25, 127, 152, 167
   B *2:* 362
   PS 74
Farsi
   A 74
   B *2:* 299
   PS 38, 74
Fate
   PS 46, 118, 138
Fatima
   A 65, 68, 69
   B *2:* 258, 263
Fatimids
   A 75, 81, 88
   B *1:* 43, 44, *2:* 239, 322,
      323

Ferdinand (of Portugal)
B *1:* 156, 157
Ferdinand (of Spain)
A 219
PS 24
Fernando I
B *1:* 98
Feudalism
A 2, 3, 20, 31, 37–39, 50,
114, 124, 129, 180, 181,
213, 221, 222
B *2:* 368
Fez
B *2:* 224
Fiammetta
B *2:* 266
Finnbogi
B *2:* 221
Finns
A 57, 99
First Amendment
A 115
First Crusade
A 91, 102–04, 106, 107,
109
B *1:* 50, 51, 151, 166, 180,
182, *2:* 324, 325, 328,
360
PS 5, 10–13, 15, 44, 118
"First Deposition and Ban-
ning of Henry IV"
B *1:* 145
PS 111–19
First Ecumenical Council
B *1:* 187
FitzGerald, Edward
B *1:* 94
"Five Dynasties and Ten
Kingdoms"
A 169
Five Years' Campaign
B *2:* 347
Flagellants
A 214, 215
Florence
A 126, 203, 218
B *1:* 91–93, 95, *2:* 233,
266
PS 129
Fontevrault
B *1:* 111
Foot-binding
A 170, 171

Forbidden City
A 173
B *2:* 339, 340 (ill.)
Fortunatus
B *1:* 27
Fortune
B *1:* 53, 55, 72, 73
PS 160
Fourth Council of Constan-
tinople
A 100
Fourth Crusade
A 121
B *1:* 182
PS 11, 21
Fourth Lateran Council
A 101
B *1:* 182
Frame story
A 71
PS 54, 73, 74, 80
France
A 4, 13, 19, 21, 23, 30, 31,
34, 37, 41, 45, 65, 89,
91–96, 100, 102, 103,
108, 109, 111, 113–17,
119, 121, 123, 124, 126,
129, 132, 156, 214, 217,
222, 225
B *1:* 1, 2, 5, 61–64, 66, 69,
70, 74, 77–79, 82, 83,
105–07, 109, 110, 113,
114, 116, 118, 124, 140,
142, 148, 173, 180–83,
2: 191–98, 213, 218,
220, 246, 247, 265, 290,
313, 314, 316, 318, 325,
326, 329, 353, 354, 365,
366, 368
PS 12, 45, 46, 82, 83, 90,
93–95, 98–100, 124,
126, 133, 145, 147, 150,
151
Franciscans
A 123
B *1:* 118, 123, 125, 183
Francis of Assisi
A 123
B *1:* **121–27**, 121 (ill.),
183, *2:* 350
Franconia
B *1:* 170

Franks
A 21, 23, 29, 30, 32, 38,
104
B *1:* 61, 63, 67, 77, 78, 80,
82, 83, 142, *2:* 321, 375
PS 2, 6, 7, 12, 15, 16, 18,
19, 21, 22, 90, 93–96,
98, 101, 111
Fredegund
B *2:* 373, 375
PS 100
Frederick I Barbarossa
A 113, 114
B *1:* 66, 169, **172–74**, 173
(ill.), *2:* 315
Frederick II
A 124, 126
B *1:* 169, **174–75**, 175
(ill.), 180, *2:* 349
Frederick III
B *2:* 247
French Revolution
PS 63, 100
Friars
A 123
B *1:* 124, 125, 183
Frisians
A 31
Fujiwara
A 177, 180
B *2:* 267, 268, 341
PS 108, 109
Fujiwara Yoshifusa
A 180
Fulbert
B *1:* 5, 6
Funan
A 152

G

Gaiseric
A 17
Galen
B *1:* 34
Galicia
B *1:* 100
Galland, Antoine
PS 79
Gallipoli
A 82

Galswintha
  B *2:* 373
  PS 100
Ganfu
  PS 35, 36
Ganges
  A 141, 142, 146
  B *1:* 10
Gao
  A 206, 207
  B *2:* 244, 249
Garden of Paradise
  A 81
Gaul
  A 17, 21
  B *1:* 77, 78, *2:* 290
Gauls
  A 7, 13, 16
  PS 2, 6–8
Gautama, Siddhartha. *See*
  Siddhartha Gautama
Gautier Sans Avoir
  A 103
  B *2:* 360
Gelasius II (pope)
  B *1:* 138
Gemara
  A 89
  B *2:* 224
Genghis Khan
  A 133–36, 138, 140, 171
  B *1:* 16, **129–35,** 129 (ill.),
    2: 209, 282, 343, 344
  PS 33
*Genji monogatari. See Tale of
  Genji*
Genoa
  A 115, 126
  B *2:* 301, 304
  PS 34, 40
Geography
  A 127, 142, 155
  B *1:* 170, *2:* 220, 221, 302
  PS 34, 40
Geometry
  A 34, 36, 72
  B *1:* 55
George (St.)
  A 24
  B *2:* 293 (ill.)
Georgia
  A 138, 139
  B *1:* 44, 134, *2:* 346

Gerbert. *See* Sylvester II
Germain
  B *2:* 291
Germanic
  A 16, 19, 21, 23, 28, 31,
    33, 34, 98
  B *1:* 53, 55, 63, 77–79, 83,
    174
  PS 149
Germans
  A 22, 47, 114, 118
  B *1:* 16, 18, 20, 86, 88,
    145, *2:* 346
  PS 116, 145
Germany
  A 19, 22, 23, 30, 34, 37,
    96, 101, 109, 118, 124,
    128, 131, 213
  B *1:* 15, 64, 66, 78, 80,
    111, 114, 146–48, 150,
    162, 169–74, 176, *2:*
    246, 247, 351
  PS 46, 47, 50, 79, 90, 111,
    112, 116, 117, 145, 147,
    152
Gesta pontificum Anglorum
  PS 146
Gesta regum Anglorum
  PS 133, **145–53**
Ghana
  A 204–05, 207, 211
  B *2:* 230, 232, 233
  PS 2, 23–25, 27, 30, 31
Ghazis
  B *2:* 276
Ghaznavids
  A 79, 146, 147
Ghibellines
  A 114, 115
  B *1:* 92
Ghurids
  A 146, 147
Gibraltar
  B *1:* 155
Giotto
  A 220
Gobi Desert
  B *2:* 299
God
  A 10, 12, 15, 16, 24, 25,
    45, 48, 52, 61–63, 65,
    66, 68, 85–87, 91, 99,
    102, 103, 108, 109, 113,

    116, 127, 136, 142, 144,
    177, 188, 190, 193, 217,
    222, 223, 225
  B *1:* 1, 2, 6, 7, 9, 18, 23,
    27–29, 48, 49, 51, 58,
    69, 73, 74, 77, 79, 80,
    87, 92, 94, 97, 102, 107,
    115, 116, 121, 123, 124,
    126, 139, 143, 145, 146,
    163, 179, 182, 186, *2:*
    191–93, 204, 205, 226,
    230, 235, 241, 257–61,
    275, 282, 289–91, 294,
    305, 306, 308, 310, 311,
    313, 318, 321, 331, 351,
    352, 354
  PS 24, 47, 59–62, 75, 78,
    85, 86, 90, 94–98, 108,
    111, 113–16, 121, 127,
    128, 131, 138, 139, 147,
    148
Go-Daigo
  B *1:* 56, 57
Godfrey of Bouillon
  A 103, 106
  B *2:* 324–25, 325 (ill.)
Godfrey the Hunchback
  B *1:* 149
Godwinesons
  B *2:* 367
Golden Horde
  A 135, 137, 138
  B *1:* 17, *2:* 210, 346
Goliath Spring
  A 136
Golpejera
  B *1:* 100
Gone with the Wind
  PS 160
The Goodman of Paris
  PS 53, 55, **81–88**
Gospels
  B *1:* 124
Gothic architecture
  A 4, 36, 111, 112, 156
Goths
  A 13, 14
  PS 136
Granada
  A 219
  B *1:* 100
Grand Canal
  A 164, 173

B *2:* 301, 358

Grand Duchy of Vladimir-
    Suzdal. *See* Vladimir
    (Russian region)

Great Khan
    A 137
    B *2:* 210–12, 214, 215,
        298, 300

Great Pyramid of Egypt
    A 193

Great Schism
    A 222, 223
    B *1:* 184
    PS 128

Great Wall
    A 13, 14, 22, 163, 173
    B *1:* 135, *2:* 300, 339, 358,
        362
    PS 38

Great Zimbabwe
    A 210

Greece
    A 1, 2, 5, 6, 12, 13, 18, 28,
        47, 48, 59, 72, 77, 108,
        119, 122, 127, 130, 201,
        202, 219, 221
    B *1:* 33, 36, 54, 65, 85, 89,
        119, 137, 161, 163, 187,
        2: 199, 291
    PS 1, 2, 5, 7, 16, 62, 91,
        113, 121, 124, 132, 135,
        138, 143, 155

Greek Orthodox Church. *See*
    Eastern Orthodox
    Church

Greenland
    A 40, 214
    B *2:* 218–22

Gregorian chants
    A 27
    B *1:* 142

Gregory I (pope; Gregory
    the Great)
    A 27
    B *1:* 40, 41, **137–43**, 137
        (ill.), 162, 178, 179, 183
    PS 113, 114

Gregory V (pope)
    B *1:* 172

Gregory VI (pope)
    B *1:* 146, 147
    PS 117

Gregory VII (pope)
    A 100
    B *1:* 19, **145–52**, 147 (ill.),
        169, 180, *2:* 324
    PS 89, 90, **111–19**

Gregory IX (pope)
    A 124
    B *1:* 174, 183

Gregory X (pope)
    B *2:* 298

Gregory XI (pope)
    A 222

Gregory of Tours
    B *1:* 77, 80
    PS 89, 90, **93–101**

Grousset, René
    B *2:* 321

Guatemala
    A 6, 185, 187

Gudrid
    B *2:* 220

Guelph-Ghibelline conflict
    A 124

Guelphs
    A 114, 115
    B *1:* 92

Guido of Arezzo
    B *2:* 353

Guide of the Perplexed
    B *2:* 226, 227

Guilds
    A 128, 129

Guinea
    A 155, 197
    B *1:* 155, 156

Guiscard, Robert. *See* Robert
    Guiscard

Gulf of Finland
    A 58

Gulf of Mexico
    B *2:* 254

Gundobad
    B *1:* 79

Gupta Empire
    A 141, 142, 146
    B *2:* 231

Gutenberg, Johannes
    A 225

Gutrum
    B *1:* 41

Guy (of Jerusalem)
    B *2:* 326

H

Haakon
    B *1:* 71

Hadrian's Wall
    A 22

Hagia Sophia
    A 54, 55, 218
    B *2:* 199, 206, 206 (ill.)
    PS 140

Hagiography
    A 48, 56

Hajj
    A 62, 67
    B *2:* 230, 246, 248, 302,
        303

Hajjaj
    A 145

Hakuh period
    A 176, 177
    PS 108

Han dynasty
    B *2:* 359
    PS 157, 160

Hangzhou
    PS 35

Hannibal
    PS 63

Han River
    B *2:* 211

Hanseatic League
    A 128
    B *1:* 71

Han Yü
    A 168, 170

Hapsburg dynasty
    A 132

Hara-kiri
    A 182

Harold (of England)
    B *2:* 365, 367, 368
    PS 146–48, 150, 152

Harsha
    A 142
    B *1:* 10, *2:* 220, 231

Harun al-Rashid
    A 37, 71
    B *1:* 98, 99, 99 (ill.), 103,
        164, 189

Hasan al-Basri
    B *2:* 308

Hasan-e Sabbah
    A 81

B *2:* 361

Hashim
B *2:* 258

Hastings (Battle of)
A 95
B *2:* 365, 368, 369
PS 146–53

Hausa
A 207
B *2:* 248

Havel, Václav
B *1:* 18

Heaven
A 20, 29, 45, 68, 172, 174
B *1:* 28, 58, 77, 91, 95,
123, *2:* 206, 253, 260,
306, 310
PS 97, 98, 105, 106, 113,
115, 116, 121, 122, 124,
155–57, 159

Hebrew
A 74, 86–88, 90, 118
B *1:* 37, 49, 162, *2:* 223,
290, 352

Hecebolus
B *2:* 204
PS 138, 140

Hegira
A 66
B *2:* 260, 261

Heian period
A 180–81
PS 65, 71, 109

Heijo
A 178

Helgi
B *2:* 221

Hell
A 29, 68, 221
B *1:* 28, 91, 93, 95, 149, *2:*
305, 306, 310
PS 61, 115, 116, 121–23,
127, 128

Héloïse
A 109
B *1:* 1, 5–7

Henry I (of England)
A 108
B *1:* 115, *2:* 369
PS 119, 146

Henry I (of France)
B *2:* 366

Henry II (of England)
A 114, 116, 119
B *1:* 105, 108, 116, *2:* 314

Henry III (of England)
B *1:* 174

Henry III (Holy Roman Emperor)
B *1:* 146–48

Henry IV (of England)
B *1:* 118

Henry IV (Holy Roman Emperor)
A 101, 102
B *1:* 19, **145–52**, 169, 172,
180, 181, *2:* 324
PS 89, 90, **111–19**

Henry V (of England)
A 217
B *2:* 192

Henry V (Holy Roman Emperor)
B *1:* 149, 151, 172

Henry VI (Holy Roman Emperor)
B *1:* 173, *2:* 313, 315, 318

Henry VI (of England)
B *2:* 192

Henry VII (of England)
A 218

Henry VIII (of England)
A 218

Henry of Anjou. *See* Henry II
(of England)

Henry the Fowler
B *1:* 170

Henry the Lion
A 114
B *1:* 173

Henry the Navigator
A 225
B *1:* **153–59**, 153 (ill.), *2:*
220, 303, 339

Henry the Young King
B *1:* 110, 117

Heraclius
A 49

Heraldry
A 108, 111

Heresy
A 8, 12, 16, 25, 100, 123,
124, 217, 224
B *1:* 7, 50, 125, 142, 183,
2: 197, 354

PS 57, 90, 93, 94, 99

Herleve
B *2:* 366

Herodotus
B *1:* 163, 164

Herzegovina
A 83

Hieroglyphics
A 186

High Middle Ages
A 24, 25, 119, 130

Hildebrand. *See* Gregory VII

Himalayas
A 166

Hinduism
A 66, 141, 142, 144, 145,
148, 152, 155
B *1:* 9, 10, 13 B *2:* 284,
285, 301

Hippo
A 15
B *1:* 23, 26, 28–30
PS 58, 62, 63

Hippodrome
A 52
B *2:* 201, 202, 204, 205

Hisdai ibn Shaprut
A 88
B *2:* 352

Historia ecclesiastica gentis
Anglorum
B *1:* 163, 163 (ill.)

Historia novella
PS 146

Historians
B *1:* **161–67**

History of the Franks
B *1:* 77
PS 90, **93–101**

Hitler, Adolf
B *1:* 21, *2:* 361
PS 50

Hittin
A 115
B *2:* 326, 327

Ho'elun
B *1:* 130

Hohenstaufen dynasty
A 109, 132
B *1:* 172

Hojo family
A 182, 183

Jamukha
 B *1:* 131–33
Janissaries
 A 82
Japan
 A 137, 163, 167, 172, 173,
  175–84, 222
 B *1:* 56, 59, *2:* 212–14,
  266–68, 271, 329–33,
  341, 342
 PS 39, 54, 65–67, 71, 72,
  79, 91, 103, 104, 106,
  108–10
Java
 A 137, 155, 157, 172
 B *2:* 214
 PS 40
Jayavarman II
 A 152
 B *2:* 284
Jayavarman VII
 A 153
 B *2:* 284, 285
Jerome (St.)
 A 28
 B *1:* 139
Jerusalem
 A 85, 88, 102, 106, 110,
  115–17, 122, 124
 B *1:* 50, 140, 175, 181,
  182, *2:* 213, 260, 310,
  316, 323, 324, 326–28,
  360, 366
 PS 10, 15, 124
Jesus Christ
 A 6, 10, 12, 24, 25, 27, 34,
  37, 40, 48, 51, 52, 54,
  66, 85, 87, 90, 91, 98,
  101, 102, 104, 113, 117,
  118, 204, 223
 B *1:* 6, 23, 24, 26, 51,
  57–59, 77, 79, 85, 87,
  121, 123, 124, 126, 139,
  140, 143, 154, 179, 184,
  2: 193, 204, 257, 260,
  261, 275, 293, 295, 309,
  314, 324, 352, 354
 PS 10, 43, 44, 94, 95,
  97–99, 113, 114, 124,
  125, 147, 148
Jews
 A 62, 65, 67, 85–92, 104,
  145, 214, 215, 219

 B *1:* 49, 51, 175, *2:*
  224–26, 258, 260, 261,
  315, 351, 361
 PS 3, 15, 24, 28, 43–51,
  124
Jihad
 A 62, 67, 106
 B *1:* 12, *2:* 248
Joachim of Fiore
 B *2:* 311
Joan of Arc
 A 217
 B *1:* 74, *2:* **191–98**, 191
  (ill.), 195 (ill.), 292
 PS 83, 87
Johannes Philoponus
 B *2:* 236
John I (of Portugal)
 B *1:* 153
John VI Cantacuzenus
  (Byzantine Emperor)
 A 82
John XII (pope)
 A 44
 B *1:* 171, 172
John XXII (pope)
 B *1:* 118
John (disciple of Jesus
  Christ)
 PS 124, 128
John (of England)
 A 115–16
 B *1:* 108, 109, 111, 111
  (ill.), 116, 180, *2:*
  314–18
John of Gaunt
 A 216
 B *1:* 118
John of Luxembourg
 B *2:* 195
Jordan
 PS 18
Journeyman
 A 122
Joust
 A 214, 223
Joy of the Snake-World
 B *2:* 231
Juan-Juan
 A 77–78
Juchen
 A 169–71, 179

Judaism
 A 62, 63, 65, 66, 78, 85,
  86, 90, 91, 168, 202
 B *2:* 258, 260, 305, 340
Judas Iscariot
 PS 124
Judeo-Christian
 A 62
Julian of Norwich
 B *2:* 309, 311, 312
Julian the Apostate
 PS 113
Julu
 PS 159
Jupiter
 A 1
 PS 94, 113
Justin
 B *1:* 56, 58, *2:* 200, 201,
  205–07
 PS 138, 139
Justinian
 A 48, 50–52, 54–56
 B *1:* 39, 44, 64, *2:*
  199–207, 199 (ill.), 203
  (ill.)
 PS 132, 135–41
Jutes
 A 22
 B *1:* 40
 PS 145

K

Kaaba
 A 65, 66
 B *2:* 258, 262
Kaesong
 A 179
Kamakura family
 B *1:* 56, 57
Kamakura period
 A 181–83
 B *2:* 341
Kamikaze
 A 183
Kammu
 A 180
Kana
 A 181
Kanem-Bornu
 A 207

Kangaba
  B *1:* 42, 43
Kaniaga
  B *1:* 42
Kao Tsu
  A 164
  B *2:* 335, 336, 371, 372
Kao Tsung
  A 168
  B *2:* 372–74
Karakorum
  A 135
Karma
  A 142, 144
Kastrioti, George. *See* Skanderbeg
Kenshi
  B *2:* 269
Kent
  A 216
Kenya
  A 208, 209
Kepler, Johannes
  B *2:* 240
Khadijah
  A 65, 66, 68
  B *2:* 258–60, 263
Khaidu
  B *2:* 213, 214
Khalji dynasty
  A 148
  B *1:* 9, 11, 14
Khan, Genghis. *See* Genghis Khan
Khan, Kublai. *See* Kublai Khan
Khanbalik
  A 134, 137, 138, 171, 172
  B *2:* 210, 213
Khazaria
  A 78, 91, 92
Khazar khanate
  A 54, 78, 91
Khmer Empire
  A 152, 153, 155, 157
  B *2:* 284
Khorasan
  A 138
Khosrow
  B *2:* 203
Kiev
  A 41, 57, 58, 99, 135
  B *1:* 15, 17, 87

Kievan Russia
  A 49, 57, 58, 91, 99
  B *1:* 15, 16, 42
Kilwa
  A 209
  B *2:* 302
Kinsay
  PS 35, 36, 41
Kirina
  B *1:* 43
Kitab al-jabr wa al-muqua-balah
  B *2:* 235, 237
Kitab mu'jam al-buldan
  B *2:* 221
Knights
  A 4–6, 37, 38, 110, 111, 114, 116–19, 124, 130, 180, 181, 214, 223
  B *1:* 15, 18, 19, 51, 80, 81, 97, 117, 182, *2:* 318, 319, 324, 325, 328
  PS 65, 71, 87, 156
Knights Hospitalers
  A 117
Knights of Malta
  A 117
Knights of St. John of Jerusalem
  A 117
Knights of the Round Table
  A 118
  B *1:* 80, 81
Knights Templars
  A 117
  B *1:* 51
Kofun period
  A 175
  B *2:* 330
  PS 103
Koguryo
  A 179
Koken
  A 179
Kongo
  A 210–11
Koran
  A 62, 63, 66, 67, 73–75
  B *2:* 226, 257, 259, 259 (ill.), 260
Korea
  A 137, 164, 167, 171, 175–77, 179, 184

  B *2:* 212, 330, 341, 342, 359, 362, 363
  PS 33, 103
Korean Peninsula
  A 133, 134, 179
  B *1:* 135
Koryo
  A 179
Kosovo
  A 82, 83, 218
  B *2:* 275, 278, 279
Kosovo Field
  A 218
  B *2:* 275, 279
Krak des Chevaliers
  A 117
Kublai Khan
  A 137–38, 171, 183
  B *2:* **209–15**, 209 (ill.), 220, 297, 298, 300, 303, 338
  PS 33, 34, 37, 39–41
"Kubla Khan"
  B *2:* 215
Kumbi-Saleh
  A 205
Kurdistan
  B *2:* 345
Kush
  A 201, 202
Kusunoki Masashige
  A 183
  B *1:* 57
Kuyuk
  A 136
  B *2:* 210
Kyoto
  A 180, 182, 183
  B *2:* 268, 270
  PS 65, 66

L

Labrador
  B *2:* 219
Lady Murasaki. *See* Murasaki Shikibu
Lady Sarashina. *See* Sarashina
Lady Yang. *See* Yang
Lagos
  B *1:* 155

Lahore
  A 147
  B *1:* 11
Lake Chudskoe
  B *1:* 18
Lake Texcoco
  A 190
  B *2:* 252
Lake Titicaca
  B *2:* 283
Lancelot
  A 118
  B *1:* 81 (ill.)
Lanfranc
  B *1:* 114
Laos
  A 154, 155
  B *2:* 285
Lao-tzu
  A 162, 165
Larissa
  PS 7, 8
Las Navas de Tolosa
  B *1:* 36
Last Supper
  A 34, 101, 118
  PS 147
László I
  B *1:* 19
Late Middle Ages
  A 213–26
  B *2:* 266
Latin
  A 13, 21, 23, 27, 29, 36,
    51, 98, 106, 108, 110,
    119, 122, 208, 221, 225
  B *1:* 36, 37, 40, 41, 54, 63,
    77, 91, 92, 94, 114, 122,
    139, 162, *2:* 291, 368
  PS 5, 11, 129, 146, 149
Latin Empire
  A 122
  PS 11
Latin Kingdom of Jerusalem
  A 106, 110
Latvians
  B *1:* 16
La Verda
  B *1:* 126
La vita nuova
  B *1:* 93
  PS 129

*Lay of the Cid. See Poema de
    mio Cid*
Le dynasty
  A 154
Leif Eriksson
  A 40
  B *2:* **217–22**, 219 (ill.)
Leifrsbudir
  B *2:* 219, 222
Le Morte D'Arthur
  A 119
Leo I (pope)
  A 16, 17
Leo III (Byzantine Emperor)
  A 53
  B *1:* 186
Leo III (pope)
  A 35
  B *1:* 64, 146, 169, 189
  PS 111
Leo IV (Byzantine Emperor)
  B *1:* 186
Leo IX (pope)
  B *1:* 146
  PS 117
Leo X (pope)
  PS 24
Leo Africanus
  A 206
  B *2:* 243
  PS 1, 2, **23–31**
León
  B *1:* 100
Leopold of Austria
  B *2:* 315, 316
Le Pallet
  B *1:* 2
Leprosy
  A 2, 5
  B *2:* 285
Lesbos
  B *1:* 190
Letter Concerning Apostasy
  B *2:* 225
"Letter to Gregory VII"
  PS **111–19**
Lhasa
  A 166
Liao
  A 169, 179
Libya
  A 48, 68
  B *2:* 248, 263, 323

PS 140, 141
Li Che
  B *2:* 374, 375
Li Chien-ch'eng
  B *2:* 336
Li Chih. *See* Kao Tsung
Li Ch'ing-chao
  A 170
Liège
  B *2:* 221
Life of Charlemagne
  B *1:* 61, 64
Lindisfarne
  A 28, 39
  B *1:* 163
Lindisfarne Gospels
  A 28
Lingua franca
  A 63, 202, 208
Linguists
  A 175
Li Po
  A 168
  B *1:* 4, 8
Li Shih-min. *See* T'ai Tsung
Li Tan
  B *2:* 374, 375
Lithuania
  A 112
  B *1:* 16
Little Zimbabwe
  A 210
Li Yüan. *See* Kao Tsu
Li Yüan-chi
  B *2:* 336
Llull, Ramon
  PS 87
Lo Kuan-chung
  PS 131, 132, 133, **155–61**
Lombard League
  A 114
  B *1:* 173
Lombards
  A 21, 23, 28, 33, 34, 90,
    98
  B *1:* 62, 63, 137, 141, 142
London
  A 39, 126, 152, 174, 216
  B *1:* 52, 119, 152, 183, *2:*
    196, 256, 278, 328
  PS 41, 86, 88, 109, 119
London Bridge
  B *2:* 196

Lord's Sepulchre. *See* Holy
    Sepulchre
Lord's Supper
    A 94
Lorenzo the Magnificent
    A 218
Lorraine
    A 96
    B *1:* 148, *2:* 247
Lothar
    B *2:* 246
Lotharingia
    B *2:* 246
Lothario
    B *1:* 178, 179
Louis VI (of France)
    B *1:* 106
Louis VII (of France)
    A 109
    B *1:* 105–07, 110, 116
Louis IX (of France; St.
    Louis)
    A 124
Louis XI (of France)
    B *2:* 246
Louis the Pious
    B *1:* 66
Lucena
    B *1:* 35
Ludwig IV
    B *1:* 113, 118
Luo Guanzhong
    PS 156
Luoyang
    A 169
    PS 157, 158
Luther, Martin
    A 224
    B *1:* 52
    PS 128
Luxembourg
    B *1:* 78, *2:* 195, 246

M

Maccabees
    PS 124, 126
Machu Picchu
    A 196
Madeira
    B *1:* 155

Madonna and Child
    A 48, 54
Magna Carta
    A 115, 131
    B *1:* 108, 109, 112
Magyars
    A 42, 45, 96
    B *1:* 171, *2:* 274
Mahayana
    A 162, 166
Mahmud II
    A 82
Mahmud of Ghazni
    A 146
Maimonides, Moses. *See*
    Moses Maimonides
Maize
    A 186, 187
Majapahit
    A 156
Majuscule
    A 30, 36
Malay Archipelago
    A 151, 155–58
Malay Peninsula
    A 155–58
Malaysia
    A 152, 157
    B *2:* 285, 301
Maldive Islands
    B *1:* 10
Mali
    A 205–06, 207, 211
    B *1:* 39, 42, 43, 45, *2:*
        229–34, 244, 245, 303
    PS 23, 29–31
Malik Shah
    A 80
    B *1:* 94
Malindi
    A 209
Malkhatun
    B *2:* 276, 277
Malory, Sir Thomas
    A 119
    B *1:* 80
Malta
    A 117
Maltese cross
    A 117
Mamluks
    A 75, 79, 81–82, 124, 136
    B *2:* 347

Manchuria
    A 169
Manchus
    A 134, 179
"Mandate of Heaven"
    A 172, 174
    PS 106, 155, 156
Mandeville, Sir John
    B *2:* 221
Mangu
    A 136, 137
    B *2:* 210
Mani
    A 65
Manichaeism
    A 65
    B *1:* 24, 25, 27, 28, 29, *2:*
        340
Manorialism
    A 20, 30
Mansa Musa
    A 205, 206
    B *1:* 10, 42, *2:* 220,
        229–34, 229 (ill.), 244,
        246, 247
    PS 30
Manzi
    PS 35, 38
Manzikert
    A 59, 80, 99
    B *1:* 44, *2:* 275
    PS 6, 142
Marco Polo. *See* Polo, Marco
Margaret of Denmark
    B *1:* 71, 71 (ill.)
Marienburg
    A 119
Markland
    B *2:* 217, 219
Marrakech
    B *1:* 32, 35
Marranos
    A 92
Marriage
    A 51, 59, 62, 65, 67, 100,
        130
    B *1:* 5, 6, 40, 42, 55,
        70–72, 79, 86, 92, 100,
        105–08, 110, 111,
        130–32, 149, 171–74,
        180, 187, 189, *2:* 193,
        200, 201, 258, 268, 277,
        307, 315, 325, 366, 367

Marseilles
PS 46, 47

Martin IV (pope)
B *1:* 140

Martin V (pope)
A 222

Mary
A 25, 48, 52, 54
B *2:* 309
PS 115

Mary-worship
A 25

Masaccio
A 220, 221

Ma Sanpao. *See* Cheng Ho

Mathematicians and scientists
B *2:* **235–42**

Matilda of Flanders
B *2:* 367

Matilda of Tuscany
B *1:* 148–50, 149 (ill.), 180
PS 118

Maurice
A 49
B *1:* 140, 141

Mauritania
A 204
B *1:* 157
PS 30

Mauryan Empire
A 141
B *2:* 236

Maya Empire
A 6, 185–90, 192, 196, 198, 199
B *2:* 281, 282, 287

Mead
A 34, 45

Meadows of Gold
B *1:* 164

Mecca
A 6, 62, 64–67, 205
B *2:* 229–32, 238, 247, 248, 258–63, 302, 303, 308, 310, 326

Medici family
A 218

Medina
A 66
B *2:* 261–63

Mediterranean
A 15, 17, 41, 61, 106, 115, 117, 201
B *1:* 154
PS 28, 47, 63

Mehmed the Conqueror
A 218

Melaka
A 156–58
B *2:* 301

The Memoirs of Usamah ibn Munqidh
PS 15–22

Mendicant
A 122, 123
B *1:* 124, 183

Mercenary
A 214, 218
B *1:* 101

Mérida
A 187, 188

Merlin
A 118
B *1:* 80

Merovech
B *1:* 78

Merovingian Age
A 19–32, 33, 34, 38, 71
B *1:* 61, 62, 78
PS 99

Merovingian art
A 30

Mesoamerica
A 185, 188, 197

Mesopotamia
A 88, 115, 136, 138
B *2:* 210

Messiah
A 86, 87

Methodius
A 55, 56
B *1:* 18, 42, **85–90**, 85 (ill.), *2:* 292

Mexica
A 190
B *2:* 252, 256

Mexico
A 6, 185, 186, 190, 192, 193
B *2:* 251–54

Mexico City
A 190, 193
B *2:* 252, 253 (ill.)

Michael VIII Palaeologus
A 122

Michael Psellus
B *2:* 353

Middle East
A 1, 5, 7, 9, 10, 25, 61, 63, 64, 74, 75, 80, 87, 92, 130, 133, 202, 205, 208
B *1:* 10, 13, 63, 94, 161, 163, *2:* 213, 227, 229, 232, 233, 235, 238, 240, 254, 278, 279, 305, 314, 321, 326
PS 16, 18, 20, 22, 27, 30, 41, 74, 75, 79, 142

Middle English
B *1:* 119
PS 151

"Middle Kingdom"
A 37

Milan
B *1:* 26
PS 58

Milvian Bridge
A 11

Minamoto
A 181, 182

Minamoto Yoritomo
A 182

Ming dynasty
A 172–74, 209
B *1:* 156, *2:* 339, 340
PS 40, 156

Minuscule
A 36

Mishnah
A 89
B *2:* 224, 226

Mishneh Torah
B *2:* 223, 225, 226, 228

Mississippi River
A 204

Mitchell, Margaret
PS 160

Moguls
A 149

Mohammed I Askia
A 206
B *2:* **243–49**

Moluccas
A 155

Mombasa
A 209

Monasticism
    A 20, 25, 45, 100
Mongolia
    A 77, 139, 169
    B *1:* 17, 129, 134, *2:* 215
    PS 33
Mongols
    A 1, 57, 80–82, 131,
        133–40, 154, 161, 166,
        171–73, 179, 183, 204,
        214, 218
    B *1:* 4, 10, 12, 13, 15–17,
        20, 21, 129, 131 (ill.)
        133–35, *2:* 209–15, 221,
        276, 277, 298, 299, 339,
        343, 344, 348
    PS 3, 33, 34, 38, 39
Monica
    B *1:* 24–26
    PS 58
Monks
    A 20, 25–28, 30, 36, 39,
        45, 71, 94, 100, 117,
        123, 166, 203
    B *1:* 6, 27, 48, 64, 138,
        142, 162, 177–79, *2:*
        298, 311
    PS 47, 149
Monophysites
    A 25
    B *2:* 204, 205
Monotheism
    A 142
Monte Cassino
    A 25–27
    B *1:* 178, 179, *2:* 350
Montezuma I
    B *2:* **251–56**
Montezuma II
    A 193, 194, 198
    B *2:* 251, 254, 255
Moors
    A 23, 31, 69, 70
    B *1:* 32, 155, 157
Moravia
    A 56
    B *1:* 86, 88, 89
Morocco
    A 69, 88, 205, 207
    B *1:* 32, 36, 101, 126, 155,
        157, 158, *2:* 220, 224,
        225, 246, 249
    PS 2, 24, 30

Moscow
    A 58, 99, 131, 135
    B *1:* 21
Moses Maimonides
    A 89, 90
    B *1:* 49, *2:* **223–28**, 223
        (ill.), 235
Mossi
    A 211
    B *2:* 245, 248
Mount Abu
    A 146
Mount Badon
    A 118
    B *1:* 80
Mount Hira
    B *2:* 259
Movable-type
    A 162, 170, 225
Mozambique
    A 209, 210
Mu'awiya
    A 68
Mudanya
    B *2:* 278
Muhammad
    A 6, 62, 64–68, 70, 73, 75
    B *1:* 32, 164, *2:* **257–64**,
        257 (ill.), 302, 306
Muhammad Ghuri
    A 147
Murad
    A 82, 83
Murad II
    B *2:* 275
Murasaki Shikibu
    A 181
    B *1:* 71, 74, 119, *2:*
        265–71
    PS 66, 67, 71, 72
Muromachi period
    A 181, 183–84
    B *1:* 57
Musa, Mansa. *See* Mansa
    Musa
Muscovy
    A 131, 219, 220
Muslims
    A 6, 31, 38, 42, 62, 66–69,
        72, 79, 88, 90, 94, 98,
        102, 104, 106, 109, 110,
        116, 119, 123, 124, 126,
        139, 144, 145, 149, 157,

        202–04, 206, 208, 209,
        219
    B *1:* 9, 11 (ill.), 16, 31, 49,
        50, 63, 97, 100, 101,
        124, 126, 151, 154–56,
        158, 166, 175, 181, 182,
        2: 213, 224, 227, 230,
        232, 238, 244, 245, 247,
        257, 259–63, 275, 276,
        302, 303, 308, 310, 314,
        317, 321–24, 326, 343,
        351, 352, 361
    PS 2, 15, 16, 20–22, 24,
        41, 44, 78, 91, 118, 142,
        147
Muslim Spain
    B *1:* 34, *2:* 303, 352
Mutapa
    A 209–10
Mysticism
    A 63, 68, 163
    B *2:* 305, 312

N

Nakatomi Kamatari
    A 177
    B *2:* 341
    PS 108
Nan-chao
    A 154. *See also* Thais
Nancy (Battle of)
    B *2:* 247
Nanjing
    A 173
    B *2:* 339
Naples
    A 98
    B *2:* 266, 267, 350, 353
Napoleon
    PS 151
Nara period
    A 175, 178, 180
    B *1:* 112
Narses
    B *2:* 203
Nasrid
    A 69
Nationalism
    A 214, 224
Native Americans
    B *2:* 217, 219

Navarre
 B *1:* 100, *2:* 315
Nazareth
 A 136
Nazi Germany
 B *1:* 21
 PS 50, 152
Neo-Confucianism
 A 170
Nepal
 A 166
Nero
 A 10
 PS 94
Nestorian Christianity
 A 25, 136, 168
 B *2:* 212, 213, 340
Nestorius
 A 25
Netherlands
 B *1:* 78, *2:* 246, 247
Neva
 B *1:* 17, 21
Nevsky, Alexander. *See*
  Alexander Nevsky
Newfoundland
 A 40
 B *2:* 219, 222
The New Life
 B *1:* 93
New Testament
 A 20, 24
 B *1:* 23, 124, 139, *2:* 291
 PS 113, 125, 128
Newton, Isaac
 B *2:* 236
New World
 A 41, 115, 185, 186, 189,
  190, 197, 219
 B *2:* 217, 222, 304
New Zealand
 A 158
 PS 151
Nicaea
 A 12, 53, 104
 B *1:* 187
Nicene Creed
 A 12
Nicephorus Bryennius
 B *1:* 166
 PS 6
Nicholas III (pope)
 PS 123

Nicholas IV (pope)
 B *1:* 140, *2:* 213
Nichomachean Ethics
 B *1:* 34
Niebelungenlied
 A 45
Nigeria
 A 207, 211
 B *2:* 243, 248
Niger River
 A 205–07
 B *1:* 43, *2:* 244, 248, 249
Nihon shoki
 B *2:* 330, 332
 PS 109
Nika Revolt
 A 52
 B *2:* 199, 201, 202, 205,
  206
Nile River
 A 68, 201
 B *2:* 239, 263
Nimbus
 A 48, 52
Nobutaka
 B *2:* 268
Norman Conquest
 A 96, 98, 106
 PS 133, 149, 151, 152
Normandy
 A 39, 41–43, 95, 96
 B *1:* 115, *2:* 365–68
 PS 133, 145, 146, 150–52
Normans
 A 41, 94–96, 98, 102, 103
 B *1:* 151, *2:* 218, 324, 328,
  349, 365, 367, 368, 370
 PS 7, 12, 133, 145–52
Norse mythology
 A 45
North Africa
 A 7, 9, 15, 17, 48, 69, 70,
  87, 88, 92
 B *1:* 32, 36, 154, 155, *2:*
  202, 204, 220, 278, 292,
  351
 PS 27, 28, 57, 58, 136,
  140
North America
 A 2
 B *2:* 217, 218, 220, 222
Northern Europe
 A 19, 34, 37

North Sea
 A 9, 28
Norway
 A 39, 42
 B *1:* 71, *2:* 217, 218, 368
Notre Dame
 B *1:* 2, 3 (ill.), 5
Novgorod
 A 41, 57, 58, 130, 219
 B *1:* 16, 18–20
Nubia
 A 201
Nur ad-Din
 B *2:* 322, 323

O

Oaxaca
 B *2:* 253
"Ocean Sea"
 PS 35, 36
"Ockham's Razor"
 A 220
 B *1:* 117
Odoacer
 A 18, 23
 B *1:* 53–55, 55 (ill.), 58
Odo of Metz
 A 35
 B *1:* 64
Oghuz
 A 78, 79
Ogodai
 A 134, 135
 B *2:* 210
Old English
 A 22
 B *1:* 41
 PS 151
Old Silk Road
 PS 74
Old Testament
 A 24, 63, 85, 86, 89, 222
 B *2:* 223, 224, 260, 291
 PS 113, 128
Oleg
 A 57
Olga
 A 57
 B *1:* 87
Olmec
 A 185–87, 189

Oman
A 64
B *1:* 164
Omar Khayyám
A 68
B *1:* 94, *2:* 227, 235
On Buildings
PS 135, 136
Onin War
A 183
On Monarchy
B *1:* 94
*On the Art of Hunting with
  Hawks*
B *1:* 175
*On the Harmony of Religion
  and Philosophy*
B *1:* 34
*On the Merits of Sinners and
  Forgiveness*
B *1:* 28
*On the Predestination of the
  Saints*
B *1:* 29
On the Virtue of Believing
B *1:* 27
Optics
B *2:* 240
Order of Chivalry
PS 87
Order of the Garter
A 119
Ordóñez, García
B *1:* 100, 101, 102
Orestes
A 18
Orkhan
A 82
B *2:* 278
Orléans
A 217
B *2:* 191, 192, 194
Ormuz
B *2:* 298, 301
Orsini family
PS 123
Osman I
A 82
B *2:* **273–79**, 273 (ill.)
Ostrogoths
A 13, 14, 23, 48, 90
B *2:* 202, 203
PS 93

Otto II (Holy Roman Emper-
  or)
B *1:* 171, 172
Otto III (Holy Roman Em-
  peror)
A 96, 97
B *1:* 169, **171–72**, *2:* 353
Ottoman Empire
A 78, 79, 83, 219
B *2:* 249, 273, 274, 275,
  277, 278, 279, 331, 344
Ottoman Turks
A 82–83, 218
PS 12
Otto of Freising
A 204
Otto the Great (Holy
  Roman Emperor)
A 45, 56, 93, 96
B *1:* 66, **169–71**, 171 (ill.)
Ovid
PS 80
Oxford University
A 18, 32, 46, 59, 75, 106
B *1:* 103, 117, 119, 152,
  159, *2:* 222, 263, 319
PS 80, 119
Oyo
A 211

P

Pachacutec
A 195
B *2:* **281–87**
Pacific Ocean
A 176
Paekche
A 176, 179
Pakistan
A 143, 145, 147
B *1:* 9–11, *2:* 220
PS 151
Palas
A 145
Palenque
A 188
Palestine
A 48, 50, 85, 86, 88, 90,
  102, 110, 115, 117, 214
B *1:* 164, 166, 174, 181, *2:*
  224, 225, 315–17, 322

PS 2, 10, 12, 15–17, 44,
  91, 118
Palladius
B *2:* 291
Pallava
A 142
B *1:* 10
Pamir
B *2:* 299
PS 40
Papal States
A 34, 98
Paradise
A 81, 221
B *1:* 94, 95, *2:* 305, 310
PS 121, 122
Paris
A 94–96, 112, 113, 126,
  152, 214, 216
B *1:* 2, 3, 7, 70, 82, 82
  (ill.), 116, 178, *2:* 195,
  239, 350, 351
PS 53, 55, 81–88
Parlement of Foules
B *1:* 118
Passover
B *2:* 224
Pataliputra
B *2:* 236
Patay
B *2:* 194
Patriarch
A 48, 51, 52
B *1:* 86, 140, 186
Patricius
B *1:* 24, 25, *2:* 289
PS 58
Patrick (St.)
A 28
B *2:* **289–95**, 289 (ill.)
Paul IV
B *1:* 186
Paul (apostle)
PS 113
B *2:* 291
Paul of Aegina
B *2:* 236
"Pax Romana"
A 7
Peace of Constance
A 114
B *1:* 173

Peasant's Crusade
  B *2:* 360
Pedro II
  B *1:* 174
Pelagians
  B *1:* 28
Pepin III
  A 33, 53
  B *1:* 62
  PS 99
Père-Lachaise
  B *1:* 7
Persia. *See also* Iran
  A 49, 61–63, 68, 71, 72,
    74, 78, 88, 136, 138
  B *1:* 24, 36, 94, 134, 156,
    157, 164, *2:* 202, 203,
    210, 213, 298, 301, 302,
    340, 345
  PS 28, 34, 38, 74
Peru
  A 194, 197
  B *2:* 282
Perugia
  B *1:* 122
Peter (apostle)
  A 10
  PS 113, 115, 124
Peter of Morrone
  B *1:* 140
Peter the Great
  B *1:* 21
Peter the Hermit
  A 103, 109
  B *2:* 360, 362
Petrarch
  A 221, 222
  B *1:* 95, *2:* 266, 267
  PS 128
Philip I (of France)
  B *2:* 368
  PS 12
Philip II Augustus (of
    France)
  A 91, 114, 115, 116
  B *1:* 181, *2:* 314
Philip IV (of France)
  A 132
  B *1:* 140, 183
Philippa of Lancaster
  B *1:* 153
Philippines
  A 155, 158, 172

Philip the Good
  B *2:* 246
Philosophy
  A 63, 68, 72, 88–90, 146
  B *1:* 1, 32–34, 49, 53,
    57–59, 86, *2:* 223, 226,
    227, 240, 268, 353
  PS 62
Phoenicia
  A 61
Physics
  B *1:* 31, 33
Piast
  A 99
Picts
  A 22
Pilgrimage
  A 62, 63, 67, 102, 103,
    205
  B *1:* 126, *2:* 213, 229, 230,
    232, 246, 247, 261, 263,
    302, 303, 310, 366
  PS 85
Pillars of Islam
  A 66
Pisa
  A 115, 126, 222
  PS 128
Pius II (pope)
  A 126
Pizarro, Francisco
  A 198
Plague. *See also* Black Death
  A 48, 49, 91, 213–15, 221
  B *1:* 70, 139, 162, *2:* 266,
    361
  PS 3, 43, 46, 47, 49, 141
Plantagenet
  B *1:* 110
Plate armor. *See also* Armor
  A 221, 223
Plato
  B *1:* 34, 54, *2:* 353
Poema de mio Cid
  B *1:* 102, 103
Poetics
  B *1:* 34
Poet's Corner
  B *1:* 119
Poitiers
  A 217
Poland
  A 56, 99, 112, 131, 135

  B *1:* 18, 19, 21
Polo, Marco
  A 81, 127, 128, 138, 156,
    158, 171, 174, 176
  B *1:* 13, *2:* 209, 212–15,
    220, 221, **297–304,** 297
    (ill.), 299 (ill.)
  PS 1, 3, **33–41,** 109
Polynesia
  A 158
Polytheism
  A 142
Ponte San Giovanni
  B *1:* 122
Pony Express
  A 195
Poor Knights of Christ
  A 117
Pope ... *See* under ruling
    names, for example, In-
    nocent III, Gregory VII,
    etc.
Porto Santo
  B *1:* 155
Portugal
  A 88, 92, 158, 211, 219,
    225
  B *1:* 32, 153–56, 158, *2:*
    303
Post-Classic period
  A 190
Predestination
  B *1:* 28, 29
Prester John
  A 136, 202, 204
  B *2:* 221
Prince Henry the Navigator.
    See Henry the Navigator
Prince Shotoku. *See* Shotoku
    Taishi
Princess's Palace
  PS 70
Priscian
  B *1:* 36
Priyadarsika
  B *2:* 231
Procopius
  A 56
  B *2:* 201, 206
  PS 131–33, **135–43**
Prokofiev, Sergei
  B *1:* 21

Prophet Muhammad. *See*
Muhammad
Protestant movement
B *1:* 52
PS 50, 153
Provence
A 108, 119
Prussia
A 96, 119
Pskov
B *1:* 16
Ptolemy
B *2:* 240
Pudmini
A 149
Pulakeśin
B *1:* 10
Pulakeśin II
B *1:* 10
Punjab
A 145
Purgatory
A 20, 29, 221
B *1:* 91, 93, 95
PS 121, 122

Q

Qasim
A 145
Quechua
A 194
B *2:* 284
Queen of Sheba
A 202
Queen Tamara. *See* Tamara
Quetzalcóatl
A 190, 192, 193
B *2:* 252
Quetzalcóatl Pyramid
A 193
Quipu
A 197
Quraish
A 65, 66
B *2:* 258
Quran. *See* Koran
Qutb-ud-Din Aybak
A 147
B *1:* 11

R

Rabban Bar Sauma. *See* Bar
Sauma, Rabban
Rabia al-Adawiyya
A 68
B *1:* 97, *2:* **305–12**
Racism
A 202, 209
PS 75
Rajaraja I
B *1:* 10
Rajendra
B *1:* 10
Rajputs
A 145
Ralph of Vermandois
B *1:* 106
Ramadan
A 67
B *1:* 11
Rambam. *See* Moses Mai-
monides
Ramón Berenguer II
B *1:* 101
Rashi
A 89
B *2:* 353
Ravenna
A 16, 35, 54
B *1:* 55, 64, *2:* 202
Raymond IV
A 103
B *2:* 325
Raymond of Toulouse
B *1:* 107
PS 13
Reconquista
A 126, 219
B *1:* 35, 37, 99
Records of Ancient Times
A 180
The Red Badge of Courage
PS 160
Red Sea
A 65, 201–04
B *2:* 258
Reformation
A 2, 3, 220, 222, 224
B *1:* 52
PS 50, 128
Reims
B *2:* 191, 193, 194

PS 95, 97
Reincarnation
A 142, 144
B *2:* 285
Remigius
PS 95, 97, 98
Renaissance
A 2–4, 35, 36, 213, 218,
220, 221
B *1:* 63, 96, 114
PS 28, 71, 81, 128, 129
The Republic
A 211
Reynaud de Chatillon
B *2:* 326
Rhazes. *See* Al-Razi
Rheims. *See* Reims
Rhetoric
B *1:* 26, 34
Rhine
A 9
B *1:* 78
PS 48
Richard I (of England; the
Lion-Hearted)
A 114, 117
B *1:* 108, 111, 111 (ill.),
116, 173, *2:* **313–19**,
313 (ill.), 321, 326
Richard I of Normandy
A 95
PS 145
Richard II (of England)
A 216
B *1:* 118, *2:* 361
Rienzi
B *2:* 361
Rienzo, Cola di
A 218
B *2:* 361
The Ring
A 45
B *2:* 277
Ripuarian Franks
B *1:* 78
Ritual suicide
A 181, 182
B *2:* 231
Rivera, Diego
B *2:* 255 (ill.)
River Neva
B *1:* 17

River Seine
A 94
B 2: 198
River Tiber
A 11
Road of Long Study
B 1: 73
Robert I of Normandy
B 2: 365
Robert de Baudricourt
B 2: 193
Robert Guiscard
A 98, 101
B 1: 151, 2: 324
PS 7, 12, 118
Robin Hood
B 2: 313, 317 (ill.), 319
Rockets
A 171
Rodrigo Díaz de Vivar. *See* El
Cid
Roman Catholic Church. *See*
Catholic Church
Romance
B 1: 72–74, 97
Romance of the Rose
A 119
B 1: 73
***Romance of the Three King-
doms***
A 163
PS 132, 133, **155–61**
Romance of Troy
A 119
Roman Empire
A 1, 3, 7–18, 19–21, 24,
28, 35, 42, 47, 48, 50,
53, 80, 96, 110, 112,
126, 130, 139, 142, 161,
219, 223
B 1: 23, 24, 29, 33, 34, 36,
53–55, 64–66, 77, 122,
123, 137, 139, 140, 146,
169, 170, 172, 173, 185,
189, 2: 199, 202, 203,
231, 232, 318, 357, 359
PS 1, 3, 5, 46, 57, 58, 90,
93, 100, 111, 132, 135,
136, 140, 145, 153
Romanesque
A 36, 111, 112
Romania
A 13

B 2: 318, 346
Romanianus
B 1: 25
Roman numerals
A 13
Roman Republic
A 7
B 1: 55
Romans
A 1, 7, 8, 10, 13–17,
21–23, 25, 35, 36, 45,
48, 85, 87, 90, 94, 162,
167, 195
B 1: 24, 29, 54, 55, 64, 65,
77, 78, 81, 114, 138,
146, 151, 169, 189, 2:
200
PS 5, 13, 62, 63, 90, 100,
111, 113, 147
Rome
A 1–11, 13–18, 20, 22–25,
28–30, 33–35, 37, 42,
45, 47, 51, 53, 59, 80,
90, 93, 98, 100–02, 108,
119, 126, 127, 130, 132,
203, 206, 218, 219,
221–23
B 1: 23–26, 28, 29, 36, 40,
41, 54, 55, 64, 65, 77,
79, 82, 88, 89, 114, 115,
124, 125, 137–40, 142,
146, 147, 150, 151, 161,
172, 178, 180, 182, 183,
2: 202, 203, 207, 213,
274, 289, 291, 292, 298,
324, 351–53, 357, 361
PS 46, 50, 58, 62, 63, 90,
91, 94, 111, 117, 124,
128, 143, 155
Romulus Augustulus
A 18
Roscelin de Compiègne
B 1: 2
Rossetti, Dante Gabriel
PS 128
Rouen
B 2: 197
Rubáiyát
B 1: 94, 2: 227
Rudolf I
A 132
Rudolf
B 1: 148–50

Runnymeade
B 1: 109
Rurik
A 57
Russia
A 41, 49, 54, 57, 58, 78,
79, 83, 91, 99, 130, 131,
134–38, 142, 219
B 1: 15–19, 21, 42, 44, 85,
87–89, 134, 2: 210, 218,
220, 278, 293, 302, 343,
346, 352
PS 33
Rusticana
B 1: 55
Rustichello
B 2: 302
PS 34

S

Sabbatius
PS 138
Sadako
PS 66
Sagres
B 1: 155, 158
Sahara Desert
A 201
B 1: 32, 2: 245
PS 3, 23
Sailendras
A 155
Saint-Denis
B 1: 6
Saladin
A 75, 115, 116
B 2: 314, 316, **321–28**,
321 (ill.), 327 (ill.)
Salah ud-Din Yusuf ibn
Ayyub. *See* Saladin
Salians
B 1: 78
Salic Law
B 1: 82
Salisbury Castle
B 1: 111
Samarkand
A 138, 139
B 2: 343–45, 347
PS 74, 76

Samuel (of Bulgaria)
A 59
B *1:* 43, 44
Samuel ha-Nagid
A 89
B *2:* 352
Samurai
A 180–84
PS 65, 71
Sanaska
B *2:* 231
Sancho
B *1:* 98–100
San Damiano
B *1:* 123
Sanskrit
A 142, 146
Santa Claus
B *2:* 292, 293
Santiago de Compostela
A 102
San Vitale
A 35, 51, 54
B *1:* 64, *2:* 202–05
PS 140, 142
Saphadin
B *2:* 316
Saracens
A 102
B *2:* 314
PS 79
Sarashina
PS 53, 54, **65–72**
Sassanid Empire
A 64
Sassanids
A 88, 202
Satan
A 15, 40
B *1:* 178, *2:* 193, 275
PS 123
Saudi Arabia
B *2:* 302
Saxons
A 22, 31, 34, 38, 95, 118
B *1:* 40, 41, 63, 80, 81,
142
PS 145, 146
Saxony
A 96, 114
B *1:* 147, 170, 173
PS 112

Scandinavia
A 39, 40
B *1:* 71, *2:* 217, 218, 293
Scholastica
A 27
B *1:* 179
Scholasticism
A 109, 129
B *1:* 117, *2:* 349
Science
A 3, 47, 72, 75, 124, 127,
130, 146, 170, 188, 189,
197, 198, 220
Scientists
B *1:* 37, *2:* 235–37, 240,
242
Scotists
A 220
Scotland
A 22, 28, 39, 222
B *2:* 196, 293
Scott, Sir Walter
B *2:* 313
Scriptures
A 29, 63, 86, 90, 176
B *1:* 49, *2:* 220, 223, 352
Scythians
A 146
Sea of Marmara
B *2:* 277
Second Council of Nicaea
A 53
Second Crusade
A 109–10
B *1:* 47, 50, 51, 107, 172,
2: 322, 326
Secret History
A 56
B *2:* 201
PS 132, **135–43**
Seine
A 94
B *2:* 198
Seljuks
A 79–83, 102, 124, 136,
146
B *1:* 39, 44, 94, *2:* 275–77,
322, 331
Seoul
A 179
Sephardim
A 86, 88, 90, 92

Seppuku
A 182
Serbia
A 55, 56, 59, 82, 218
B *1:* 18, 88, *2:* 274, 275
**"Seventeen-Article Consti-
tution"**
A 176
B *2:* 329, 331
PS **103–10**
Seventh Crusade
A 124
Seventh Ecumenical Council
A 53
B *1:* 185, 187
Shahrazad
A 71
PS 54, 73–75, 77–80
Shahriyar
A 71
PS 54, 74–79
Shakespeare, William
A 217
B *2:* 269
PS 121
Shang dynasty
A 161
Shang-tu
B *2:* 215, 300
Sheherazade
PS 80
Shi'ite Muslims
A 62, 63, 68
Shikibu, Murasaki. *See*
Murasaki Shikibu
Shinto
A 176–78
B *2:* 329, 330
PS 67, 68, 91, 103, 104
Shirkuh
B *2:* 322, 323
Shlomo Yitzhaqi. *See* Rashi
Shomu
A 179
Shotoku Taishi
A 176
B *2:* 275, **329–33**, 329
(ill.), 341
PS 89, 91, **103–10**
Siberia
A 166
Sicily
A 42, 49, 98, 214, 222

B *1:* 44, 138, 151, 173–75,
    2: 202, 218, 220, 315
PS 12, 118, 141
Siddhartha Gautama
    A 143, 144, 155, 163
    B *2:* 330
    PS 103, 105, 106
Silesia
    A 135
Silk Road
    B *2:* 340
    PS 74
Silla
    A 179
Simeon Stylites
    B *1:* 27, 179
Simon Magus
    PS 128
Simon of Brie
    B *1:* 140
Simony
    A 94, 99
    B *1:* 142, 181
    PS 117, 121–23, 126, 128
Sinbad
    A 71
    PS 54, 73, 75, 79, 80
Sind
    A 145
Singapore
    A 157
Sixth Crusade
    A 124, 126
    B *1:* 174, 175
Skanderbeg
    A 83
    B *2:* 275
"Skraelings"
    A 41
    B *2:* 220, 221
Slavs
    A 41, 47, 49, 54, 57, 60,
    78, 96, 99
    B *1:* 86, 89
Slovakia
    A 56
Slovenia
    A 56
Soga clan
    A 176
    B *2:* 331, 341
    PS 103, 108

Soissons
    B *1:* 6, 78
    PS 93–97
Solomon
    A 117, 130, 202
Songhai
    A 206–07, 211
    B *2:* 231, 233, 243–45,
    248, 249
    PS 23, 30
"A Song of Pure Happiness"
    B *1:* 4
Song of Roland
    A 119
    B *1:* 63
    PS 147, 148
Song of Solomon
    A 130
Soninke
    B *2:* 244
Sonni Ali
    A 206
    B *2:* 244, 245
South Africa
    PS 151
South America
    A 158, 185
    B *2:* 281
South China Sea
    A 151
Southeast Asia
    A 75, 142, 151–59, 167
    B *1:* 10, 14, 156, *2:* 300,
    301, 303
Southern Sung
    A 169
    B *2:* 339
South Seas
    A 158
Southwest Asia
    A 136, 137
    B *2:* 210
Soviet Union
    A 139
    B *1:* 18, 21
    PS 79
Spain
    A 17, 19, 23, 31, 34, 42,
    48, 69, 70, 72, 75, 86,
    88–90, 92, 102, 112,
    117, 119, 126, 158, 198,
    218, 219, 222, 225

B *1:* 29, 31, 32, 34–36, 49,
    63, 98, 101, 102, 124,
    125, 142, 154, 174, 181,
    2: 203, 220, 224, 265,
    303, 315, 351, 352
PS 24–26, 87, 93, 140, 147
Spanish Inquisition
    A 219
Spontaneous generation
    A 40
Squire
    A 108, 117
Sri Lanka. *See* Ceylon
Srivijaya
    A 155, 157
Srong-brt-san-sgam-po
    A 166
Ssu-ma Kuang
    A 170
    B *1:* 161, **164–66,** *2:* 338
Stalin, Josef
    B *1:* 15, 21
Stamford Bridge
    B *2:* 368
St. Andrew. *See* Andrew
St. Anselm of Canterbury.
    See Anselm of Canter-
    bury
St. Augustine. *See* Augustine
St. Bede the Venerable. *See*
    Venerable Bede
St. Benedict. *See* Benedict
St. Columba. *See* Columba
St. Cyril. *See* Cyril
St. Dominic. *See* Dominic
Stephen I (of Hungary)
    B *1:* 19
Stephen (of England)
    B *1:* 109
Stephen Dusan
    B *2:* 275
Steppes
    A 133, 134
    B *1:* 130
St. Francis of Assisi. *See* Fran-
    cis of Assisi
St. George. *See* George
St. Gregory. *See* Gregory I
Stilicho
    A 16

St. Jerome. *See* Jerome

St. Louis. *See* Louis IX

St. Methodius. *See* Methodius

Stoicism
B *1:* 58

Stoker, Bram
B *2:* 346

Story of My Misfortunes
B *1:* 7

Story of the Water Margin
PS 156, 161

St. Patrick. *See* Patrick

St. Patrick's Day
B *2:* 289, 292

St. Paul. *See* Paul (apostle)

St. Peter. *See* Peter (apostle)

St. Petersburg
B *1:* 21

Strasbourg
PS 43–50

St. Valentine. *See* Valentine

Sudan
A 201, 203–07, 211

Sufism
A 68
B *2:* 305–07, 310, 312

Sui dynasty
A 163–64
B *2:* 335, 357, 358, 363
PS 161

Suiko
B *2:* 331
PS 104

Sultanate of Rum
A 80

Sumanguru
B *1:* 42, 43

Sumatra
A 155, 156
B *2:* 301

Sumer
A 61

Summa contra gentiles
B *2:* 351

Summa theologica
B *2:* 349, 351–53

Sundiata Keita
A 205
B *1:* 39, 42–43, 43 (ill.), 45, *2:* 230, 232

Sun dynasty
PS 160

Sung dynasty
A 134, 169–71
B *1:* 164, *2:* 210, 338, 339

Sunni Muslims
A 79

Superstition
A 40, 71, 107
B *2:* 236

Suryavarman II
A 152
B *2:* 284

Sutras
PS 68, 70

Swabia
B *1:* 148, 170
PS 112, 116, 117

Swahili
A 208

Sweden
A 39, 41, 42, 57
B *1:* 71

Switzerland
A 19
B *2:* 247

Syagrius
B *1:* 78

Sylvester II (pope)
B *1:* 19, 172, *2:* 353

Symmachus
B *1:* 54, 55

Syria
A 48, 50, 61, 65, 72, 81, 88, 104, 106, 115, 117, 136
B *1:* 27, 36, 44, 140, 181, *2:* 204, 220, 258, 321–24, 343, 347
PS 12, 15, 16, 141

T

Tagaste
B *1:* 24–26, 30
PS 58, 64

Taiho
A 178, 181

Taika Reforms
B *2:* 341

Taishi, Shotoku. *See* Shotoku Taishi

T'ai Tsung
A 164, 165, 167, 168

B *2:* **335–42**, 335 (ill.), 357, 359, 372

Talas
A 168
B *2:* 342

Tale of Genji
A 181
B *2:* 265, 268–71
PS 65–67, 71, 72

Tale of the Rose
B *1:* 73

Talmud
A 88, 89
B *2:* 224, 226, 352, 353

Tamara
A 139

Tamerlane
A 83, 138–39, 148, 149, 220
B *1:* 10, 13, 97, *2:* 278, **343–48**, 343 (ill.)

Tamils
B *1:* 10

Tancred
A 103, 106
B *2:* 324, 325

T'ang dynasty
A 163, 164–69, 177
B *1:* 4, *2:* 220, 335, 336, 338, 341, 357, 360, 361, 374, 375
PS 67, 109

Tangier
B *1:* 157, *2:* 302

Tanzania
A 208, 209

Taoism
A 162, 165
B *1:* 4
PS 156, 161

Tao te Ching
PS 157

Tara
B *2:* 293, 294

Targutai
B *1:* 130

Tatars
A 135
B *1:* 130, 132

Tauresium
B *2:* 200

Tbilisi
A 139

Tebaldo Visconti. *See* Gregory X (pope)
Technology
A 2, 4, 38, 110, 111, 134, 170, 194
B 2: 240–42, 252, 337
Tegaza
PS 26, 28
Temmu Restoration
A 183
Templars
A 117
B 1: 51
Temujin
A 133
B 1: 129–31
Tenchi
A 177, 178, 180
B 2: 341
PS 108, 109
Tenochtitlán
A 190–92
B 2: 252, 253
Teotihuacán
A 185, 186, 190
Terrorists
B 2: 316
Teutonic Knights
A 118, 130
B 1: 15, 19
Texcoco
A 190, 192
B 2: 252
Thailand
A 152, 154, 158
B 2: 285, 301
Thais
A 154, 155. *See also* Nanchao
Thar Desert
A 142
Theobald
B 1: 116
Theodora
A 52, 54, 56
B 2: 199–202, 202 (ill.), 204–07
PS 132, 136–42
Theodoric
A 23
B 1: 55, 56, 58, 58 (ill.)
Theology
A 86, 108

B 1: 59, 163, 2: 351
Theophano
B 1: 171, 172
Third Crusade
A 114–17
B 1: 108, 111, 173, 2: 313, 315, 317, 321
PS 21
Third Punic War
PS 63
Third Rome
A 219
Thomas Aquinas
A 129
B 1: 117, 2: **349–55**, 349 (ill.)
Thor
A 45
Thorfinn
B 2: 220
Thoros
B 2: 325
Thorstein
B 2: 220
Thorvald
B 2: 219, 220
The Thousand and One Nights
A 71
B 1: 103
PS 53, 54, **73–80**
Thuringia
B 1: 170, 174
Tibet
A 137, 165, 166, 169, 172
B 2: 214, 300, 301, 303
Tibetan Buddhism
A 166
Tikal
A 187, 188
Timbuktu
A 206
B 2: 232, 243, 245, 248
PS 2, 23–31
Timur Lenk. *See* Tamerlane
Tlacaelel
B 2: 254
Tlatelóco
A 192
Toghril Beg
A 79
B 2: 275, 329, 331

Toghrul
B 1: 131–33
Toledo
A 69
B 1: 35, 36, 101
Tolstoy, Leo
B 2: 269
Toltecs
A 190
Tomislav
B 2: 274
Tonsure
A 94, 100
Topa
A 195
B 2: 286, 287
Torah
A 87
B 2: 223, 225, 226, 228
Tours
A 31, 38
B 1: 77, 80
PS 89, 90, 93–95, 99, 101
Trabzon
B 2: 301
Trade
A 51, 64, 103, 126–29, 144, 146, 157, 158, 172, 202–04, 207–09, 211, 214
Tran dynasty
A 153
Transubstantiation
A 101, 223
Transylvania
B 1: 19, 2: 346
Travel
A 103, 127, 171, 195, 214
B 1: 86, 116, 126, 2: 218, 220, 286, 297, 301
Travels of Ibn Battuta
B 2: 303
The Treasure of the City of Ladies
B 1: 74
PS 81–88
Treaty of Verdun
A 37
B 1: 66, 2: 246
Treaty of Winchester
B 1: 109
Trebizond
A 122